Every Kid's Guide to
Intelligent Spending

Written by
JOY BERRY

CHILDRENS PRESS ®
CHICAGO

About the Author and Publisher

Joy Berry's mission in life is to help families cope with everyday problems and to help children become competent, responsible, happy individuals. To achieve her goal, she has written over two hundred self-help books for children from infancy through age twelve. Her work has revolutionized children's publishing by providing families with practical, how-to, living skills information that was previously unavailable in children's books.

Joy has gathered a dedicated team of experts, including psychologists, educators, child developmentalists, writers, editors, designers, and artists to form her publishing company and to help produce her work.

The company, Living Skills Press, produces thoroughly researched books and audiovisual materials that successfully combine humor and education to teach children subjects ranging from how to clean a bedroom to how to resolve problems and get along with other people.

Managing Editor: Ellen Klarberg
Copy Editors: Kate Dickey, Annette Gooch
Contributing Editors: Libby Byers, Yoná Flemming, Susan Motycka
Editorial Assistant: Lana Eberhard

Art Director: Laurie Westdahl
Designer: Laurie Westdahl
Illustration Designer: Bartholomew
Inking Artist: Susie Hornig
Coloring Artist: Susie Hornig
Lettering Artist: Linda Hanney
Production Artist: Gail Miller

Typographer: Communication Graphics

Anyone who spends money on products or services is a consumer.

In **Every Kid's Guide To Intelligent Spending**, you will learn

- what manufacturers, merchants, and consumers do;
- how manufacturers and merchants use advertising to sell their products;
- how manufacturers and merchants use packaging, displays, and bargains to sell their products;
- how to purchase products intelligently;
- how to return unwanted products; and
- how to purchase mail-order products.

A *manufacturer* is a person or company who makes products for people to buy.

A **merchant** is a person who sells products to people.

A *consumer* is a person who buys and uses the products made by the manufacturers and sold by the merchants.

Most consumers your age spend money on things such as:

food	gifts
beverages	clothes
toys	magazines
games	books
equipment	records
recreation	cassettes
entertainment	school supplies

Most consumers your age purchase products
- at stores,
- through the mail,
- from salespeople, or
- from friends and acquaintances.

To persuade consumers to buy its product, a
manufacturer often tries to convince them
- that consumers want or need the products and
- that the manufacturer's products are the best.

To persuade consumers to buy, a merchant often tries to convince them

- that the merchant's prices are fair and
- that consumers should buy from the merchant.

Some manufacturers and merchants use ***advertising*** to persuade consumers to buy their products. The purpose of advertising is to
- get the attention of a consumer,
- let the consumer know a product is available, and
- motivate the consumer to buy a product.

One kind of advertising is **_printed advertising._** It includes

- advertisements in the Yellow Pages of a telephone book,
- magazine ads, and
- newspaper ads.

A second kind of advertising is **broadcast advertising.**
It includes
- radio commercials and
- television commercials.

A third kind of advertising is **outdoor advertising.** It includes
- signs,
- posters, and
- billboards.

Signs and posters displayed on buses, trains, taxis, and trucks are called **transit advertisements.**

A fourth kind of advertising is ***direct-mail advertising.*** It includes
- brochures,
- fliers,
- catalogs,
- order forms,
- magazine ads, and
- newspaper ads.

This kind of advertising has information about products that can be ordered and delivered by mail.

A fifth kind of advertising is **_gimmick advertising._**
It includes

■ skywriting,

■ special events, and

■ hot-air balloons.

It also includes things that have advertising on them,
such as pens, pencils, balloons, shopping bags, and
other items.

There are many **advertising techniques** used in the various kinds of advertising. One advertising technique uses **musical jingles.**

Some manufacturers and merchants use songs to tell about their products. The songs are fun to sing and easy to remember so that consumers will be encouraged to sing them and think about the products.

A second kind of advertising technique uses *catchy slogans.*

Some manufacturers and merchants use simple sayings to tell about their products. The slogans are clever and easy to remember so that consumers will be encouraged to repeat them and think about the products.

A third advertising technique uses ***personal endorsements.***

Some manufacturers and merchants pay famous people to say they like certain products so that ordinary people who admire these famous people will want to buy the products.

Other manufacturers and merchants have ordinary people say good things about their products so that other ordinary people will think the product is good enough to buy.

A fourth advertising technique is ***to promise that the consumer will save money.***

Some manufacturers and merchants try to convince consumers that they can save money by buying their products.

A fifth advertising technique is **to invite the consumer to "join the crowd."**

Some manufacturers and merchants try to convince consumers that everyone buys their products and that any person who does not will feel "left out."

A sixth advertising technique is **_to use big words._**

Some manufacturers and merchants use big words to describe their products so consumers will think that what is being said about the product is scientifically true.

Other advertising gimmicks are used by manufacturers and merchants to try to persuade consumers to believe the following:

■ The product is better than any other product like it.

■ The product will make the consumers more beautiful, more successful, or more popular.

■ The product will make life easier, better, or more fun and exciting.

In addition to advertising, manufacturers and merchants use packaging, displays, and bargains to persuade consumers to buy their products.

Packages are the containers in which products are sold. Sometimes manufacturers use larger-than-necessary packages to make products look bigger than they are.

Sometimes manufacturers use attractive pictures, colors, or wording on packaging to make products seem better than they are.

Displays are exhibits that attract attention to products.

Sometimes merchants use displays to make products look better than they are.

Bargains are products selling for reduced or lower-than-usual prices.

Products sold as bargains are usually
- *as is* (damaged)
- *seconds* (not of the best quality)
- *irregulars* (flawed)
- *special purchases* (purchased in large quantities so that the merchant can sell them for a lower price)
- *out of style* (not up to date)
- *out of season* (not usable right away because the time to use them has passed)
- *obsolete* (no longer manufactured)

Sometimes merchants use bargains to persuade consumers to buy their products.

The goal of manufacturers and merchants is to sell their products.

The goal of consumers is to *get their money's worth* when buying products. When consumers get their money's worth, they pay fair prices to purchase good-quality products they really need or want.

You can get your money's worth by doing the
following:

- Avoid *impulse spending,* which is spending money
  hastily without thinking.
- Get to know the merchant, the price, and the
  product or service *before* you spend your money.

Get to know the merchant. Find out whether the merchant sells good-quality products at fair and honest prices. Also find out whether the merchant gives good service.

You can get this information by

- talking to other people who have purchased products from the merchant and
- visiting other merchants who sell the same product.

A good merchant
- does not sell inferior products or services,
- tries to help you get exactly what you need or want, and
- replaces any product that does not work properly and exchanges it for another one or gives you back your money if you decide you do not want to keep the product you purchased.

Get to know the prices. Find out whether the price of a certain product is fair. You can get this information by
- checking the prices listed in magazine ads, newspaper ads, and catalogs;
- calling or visiting different stores; and
- talking to people who have purchased the product.

You might be fortunate enough to find the product you want **on sale.** This means the product is priced lower than usual.

It is important that you examine a sale item carefully before you buy it because it might be damaged. Make sure the item is something you will use and that it will do what you expect it to do.

Get to know the product. Find out

- if the product contains anything that can possibly harm you,
- if the product contains something you might not like, and
- exactly how much product is contained in the package.

You can get this information by doing the following:

■ Examine *food and beverages* carefully before you buy them. Read the labels on packaged food or beverages.

■ Talk to merchants who sell prepared food and beverages.

Avoid buying products

■ that do not have labels with the information you need to have about the product and

■ that are sold by merchants who are not willing to give you this information.

Examine **toys, games, and equipment** before you buy them. Make sure they
- are safe,
- can be cleaned,
- are fireproof,
- are non-allergenic, and
- aren't poisonous.

Asking yourself these questions can help you decide whether you should purchase the item:
- Is it built to withstand a normal amount of use?
- Will it do what it is supposed to do?
- Am I old enough and skilled enough to use the item on my own?
- Is it something I really want?
- Do I have my parents' or guardians' permission to make this purchase?

Carefully consider each **recreational activity** before you pay for it. Getting answers to these questions can help you decide whether you should spend your money on an activity:

- Is the activity something my parents or guardians will allow me to do?
- Is it suitable for people my age?
- Will the activity have a positive effect on me?
- Is it something I will appreciate and enjoy?

Examine *clothes* before you buy them. Select clothes that
- are well made,
- can withstand a normal amount of wear,
- can be machine-washed and tumbled dry, and
- fit you well.

Carefully consider **_magazines, books, records, and tapes_** before you buy them. Asking yourself these questions can help you decide whether or not you should purchase the item:

■ Is this something my parents or guardians would want me to buy?

■ Is it suitable for people my age?

■ Is this something that will have a positive effect on me?

■ Is this something I will understand and enjoy?

Sometimes you might want to **_return a product_** because

- it breaks easily,
- it doesn't work properly,
- it doesn't fit properly,
- it isn't what you thought it was, or
- it is something you have changed your mind about and don't want to keep.

To return a product, you need to have these four things:

■ **Sales receipt** (the piece of paper that shows what you bought and how much you paid for it)
■ **Tags** (the pieces of paper, cardboard, or plastic that are attached to a product and that give information about it)
■ **Container** (the box, plastic bag, or other packing material that holds the product)
■ **Guaranty or warranty** (the manufacturer's written promise to replace the product if it does not do what it is supposed to do)

If you decide to return a product, you need to

- gather together the product, sales receipt, tags, container, and guaranty;
- return to the place where you purchased the product;
- talk to a sales clerk, a customer service agent or representative, or a store manager;
- explain politely and honestly why you wish to return the product; and
- give the person you talk to the product, tags, container, and guaranty.

In almost every situation a merchant is usually willing
to make an exchange or give your money back if you
- return the product in a reasonable amount of time,
- have a good reason for returning the product, and
- are courteous about returning the product.

Ask your parents to help you if a merchant does not allow you to return a product.

The law is in your favor. It states that children can cancel almost any contract they make. This means that a person who sells you a product must give you back your money if you want to return the product. This also means that you can get back any item you have sold if you return the money you received for it.

Even though the law is in your favor, this does not mean you should make careless decisions.

If you want people to trust and respect you, you must be a person worthy of trust and respect. This means you should not enter into a contract or agreement with another person unless you intend to keep your part of the deal.

Sometimes you might receive an ***unsolicited product*** through the mail. This is a product mailed to you without your asking for it.

To return an unsolicited product,
- write "refused" or "return to sender" on the outside of the package and
- mail it back to the sender.

If you do not open the package, you do not have to pay the postage to mail it back to the sender.

If you open the package, you have to pay the postage to return it to the sender.

If you open the package but do not want to pay the
postage to return it, you can set it aside for a
reasonable amount of time. If the sender does not
request that the package be returned, you can do
whatever you wish with it. You do not have to pay for
anything sent to you without your asking for it.

Sometimes you might wish to purchase a product that is to be mailed to you. If you do this, it is important that you

- know the merchant, the price, and the product before you buy something through the mail; and
- use checks or money orders to pay for the product. (Do not send cash through the mail.)

Sometimes you might send a merchant a check or money-order but not receive the product. If this should happen, there are several things you should do. Keep these things:

- a copy of the order form or letter you sent to ask for the product,
- the money-order receipt or cancelled check, and
- any brochures, pamphlets, or anything else used to advertise the product.

Wait six to eight weeks. If the product hasn't come during that time, do the following:

- Call or write to the merchant. Find out whether your order was received and ask when the product will be sent to you.
- If the merchant received your money but refuses to send the product, go to your local post office and ask for help. Be sure to take the items you kept (such as the order form and cancelled check).

I ORDERED THIS TOY THROUGH THIS CATALOG OVER 12 WEEKS AGO, AND I STILL HAVEN'T RECEIVED IT!

Manufacturers, merchants, and consumers can all benefit when consumers spend their money intelligently.